101 Cozy CASSEROLES

Peg's Tomato-Bacon Pie, page 73

Warm & Wonderful Chicken Salad, page 85

Cheesy Vegetable Casserole, page 97

Gooseberry Patch
2500 Farmers Dr., #110
Columbus, OH 43235

www.gooseberrypatch.com
1·800·854·6673

Copyright 2012, Gooseberry Patch 978-1-61281-055-3
Second Printing, June, 2012

Gooseberry Patch *cookbooks*

Since 1992, we've been publishing our own country cookbooks for every kitchen and for every meal of the day! Each title has hundreds of budget-friendly recipes, using ingredients you already have on hand in your pantry.

In addition, you'll find helpful tips and ideas on every page, along with our hand-drawn artwork and plenty of personality. Their lay-flat binding makes them so easy to use...they're sure to become a fast favorite in your kitchen.

Hearty Stuffed Pepper Casserole, page 34

Baked Chicken Jambalaya, page 59

Call us toll-free at
1·800·854·6673
and we'd be delighted to tell you all about our newest titles!

Shop with us online anytime at
www.gooseberrypatch.com

Send us your favorite recipe!

and the memory that makes it special for you! If we select your recipe for a brand-new **Gooseberry Patch** cookbook, your name will appear right along with it...and you'll receive a FREE copy of the book!

Submit your recipe on our website at
www.gooseberrypatch.com

Or mail to:
Gooseberry Patch • Attn: Cookbook Dept.
2500 Farmers Dr., #110 • Columbus, OH 43235

*Please include the number of servings and all other necessary information!

Have a taste for more?

Visit **www.gooseberrypatch.com**
to join our **Circle of Friends**!

- Free recipes, tips and ideas plus a complete cookbook index
- Get special email offers and our monthly eLetter delivered to your inbox
- Find local stores with **Gooseberry Patch** cookbooks, calendars and organizers

Crustless Pizza Quiche, page 10

Broccoli Supreme, page 64

Hamburger Stroganoff Casserole, page 60

Apple-Pork Chop Casserole, page 61

Buffalo Chicken Quinoa Casserole, page 42

Zucchini Boats, page 41

Family-Favorite Corn Soufflé, page 65

CONTENTS

Harvest Casserole, page 33

Dedication

For everyone who finds comfort in enjoying a meal with family & friends.

Appreciation

Endless thanks to those talented cooks who sent us their most treasured casserole recipes!

Johnny Marzetti, page 40

Pizza Potato Puff Casserole

1 lb. ground beef
1/4 c. onion, chopped
10-3/4 oz. can cream of
   mushroom soup
8-oz. can pizza sauce
12 to 15 slices pepperoni
1/2 c. green pepper, chopped
1 c. shredded mozzarella cheese
16-oz. pkg. frozen potato puffs

Brown beef and onion in a skillet over medium-high heat; drain. Stir in soup. Spoon beef mixture into an 8"x8" baking pan that has been lightly sprayed with non-stick vegetable spray. Spoon pizza sauce evenly over beef mixture; arrange pepperoni and green pepper over sauce. Sprinkle with cheese; arrange potato puffs over top. Cover with aluminum foil; bake at 375 degrees for 30 minutes. Uncover; bake an additional 15 to 20 minutes, until heated through. Serves 4.

Gladys Kielar
Perrysburg, OH
Friday night is pizza night at our house...sometimes our family enjoys this version for variety.

Pork Chop Potato Bake

1 T. oil
6 boneless pork chops
seasoned salt and pepper to taste
1 c. shredded Cheddar cheese,
    divided
10-3/4 oz. can cream of
    mushroom soup
1/2 c. milk
1/2 c. sour cream
28-oz. pkg. frozen diced
    potatoes with onions and
    peppers, thawed
1 to 2 T. onion soup mix

Heat oil in a skillet over medium-high
heat. Season pork chops with salt and
pepper; brown in oil for 5 minutes
per side, until golden. In a bowl,
combine 1/2 cup cheese and
remaining ingredients. Spread cheese
mixture in a greased 13"x9" baking
pan. Arrange pork chops over top.
Bake, covered, at 350 degrees for
40 minutes. Top with remaining
cheese. Bake, uncovered, for an
additional 10 minutes, or until
cheese is melted. Serves 6.

Jackie Flood
Geneseo, NY
This is one of those dishes
where the leftovers can
taste even better!

Chicken Kiev Casserole

12-oz. pkg. wide egg noodles,
  uncooked
1/4 c. butter, softened
1 t. garlic powder
1 T. fresh parsley, chopped
1 deli roast chicken, cubed,
  divided and juices reserved
2 c. frozen peas, thawed
1 c. whipping cream
paprika to taste
Optional: additional fresh
  parsley

Cook noodles according to package directions until just tender; drain and set aside. In a bowl, combine butter, garlic powder and parsley. Use one teaspoon of butter mixture to grease a 13"x9" baking pan. Layer half the chicken, half the noodles and all the peas; dot with half the remaining butter mixture. Repeat layers with remaining chicken, noodles and butter mixture. Pour reserved chicken juices and cream over top; sprinkle with paprika. Bake, uncovered, at 350 degrees for 30 minutes, or until hot and bubbly. Sprinkle with parsley, if using. Serves 6.

9

John Alexander
New Britain, CT
This savory, classic dish is so good re-imagined as a casserole.

Crustless Pizza Quiche

1/2 c. pepperoni, diced
8-oz. can sliced mushrooms,
  drained
5 eggs, beaten
3/4 c. milk
1/8 t. dried oregano
1/8 t. dried basil
8-oz. pkg. shredded mozzarella
  cheese

Layer pepperoni and mushrooms in
a greased 9" pie plate. In a bowl,
whisk together eggs, milk and
seasoning; pour over pepperoni and
mushrooms. Top with cheese. Bake,
uncovered, at 400 degrees for 20 to
25 minutes, until golden and heated
through. Serves 4 to 6.

Amy Hunt
Traphill, NC
This quiche goes well
with a salad for
a quick supper!

Easy Chicken Pot Pie

2 8-oz. cans chicken, drained
2 13-1/4 oz. cans mixed
   vegetables, drained
2 10-3/4 oz. cans cream of
   chicken soup
1 c. milk
salt and pepper to taste
8-oz. pkg. shredded Cheddar
   or Colby cheese, divided
12-oz. tube refrigerated biscuits

In a bowl, combine all ingredients except cheese and biscuits. Transfer to a greased 13"x9" baking pan; top with 3/4 of cheese. Separate biscuits and tear each into 4 to 5 pieces; place on top of cheese. Sprinkle with remaining cheese. Bake, uncovered, at 350 degrees for 45 minutes, or until biscuits are golden. Serves 4.

Lynne Gasior
Struthers, OH

This is also a great way to use up leftover chicken or a rotisserie chicken.

Ravioli Lasagna

1 lb. ground beef
1 onion, diced
26-oz. jar pasta sauce, divided
25-oz. pkg. frozen cheese ravioli,
  divided
1-1/2 c. shredded mozzarella
  cheese, divided

In a skillet over medium heat, brown beef with onion; drain. In a greased 11"x7" baking pan, layer one cup pasta sauce, half the frozen ravioli, half the beef mixture and half the cheese. Repeat layering with one cup pasta sauce and remaining ravioli and beef mixture. Add remaining pasta sauce. Bake, uncovered, at 425 degrees for 30 to 35 minutes. Top with remaining cheese and bake until melted, about 5 minutes. Serves 4 to 6.

Denise Moloney
Brooksville, FL

This super-simple dish was one of my mom's favorites...everytime I make it I think of her.

Hamburger Noodle Casserole

16-oz. pkg. wide egg noodles,
  uncooked
1-3/4 lbs. lean ground beef
1 onion, chopped
1 green pepper, chopped
1 t. salt
1 t. pepper
26-oz. can cream of mushroom
  soup
12-oz. pkg. shredded Cheddar
  cheese

Cook noodles according to package
directions. Drain; set aside.
Meanwhile, in a skillet over medium
heat, brown beef with onion, green
pepper, salt and pepper; drain.
Combine beef mixture, noodles
and soup. Pour into a greased
13"x9" baking pan; top with cheese.
Bake, uncovered, at 325 degrees for
10 to 15 minutes, until cheese is
melted and bubbly. Serves 6 to 8.

13

Gloria Kirkland
Pearson, GA

This is a quick & easy recipe
that uses basic ingredients,
comes together in a snap
and tastes so good.

Quick Tuna Casserole

2 6-oz. cans tuna, drained
10-3/4 oz. can cream of
   mushroom soup
3/4 c. milk
1 T. Worcestershire sauce
hot pepper sauce to taste
1 sleeve round buttery crackers,
   crushed

In a bowl, mix together all ingredients
except crackers; set aside. In a
greased 9"x9" baking pan, layer
one-third of crackers and top with
half of tuna mixture. Repeat layers;
top with remaining crackers and
more hot sauce, if desired. Bake,
uncovered, at 350 degrees for
30 minutes, or until hot and bubbly.
Serves 4.

Debbi Corlew
Colona, IL
I grew up eating this meal,
and it's still one of my
all-time favorites.

Gnocchi Casserole

1 lb. ground pork sausage
16-oz. pkg. frozen gnocchi
26-oz. jar pasta sauce
1-1/2 t. Italian seasoning
2 c. shredded mozzarella cheese,
    divided

Brown sausage in a skillet over
medium heat; drain. Meanwhile,
cook gnocchi according to package
directions; drain. In a greased
2-quart casserole dish, combine all
ingredients except one cup cheese.
Bake, uncovered, at 350 degrees for
25 minutes, or until heated through.
Top with remaining cheese and bake
for another 10 minutes, or until
cheese is melted. Serves 4.

15

Chad Rutan
Gooseberry Patch

I love this authentic taste
of an Italian restaurant
right from my oven!

Cheesy Shrimp Casserole

8-oz. pkg. wide egg noodles, uncooked
2 4-1/4 oz. cans tiny shrimp, drained
10-3/4 oz. can cream of shrimp or cream of celery soup
3/4 c. milk
1/2 c. mayonnaise
1/4 c. celery, diced
1 t. salt
1 T. green onion, chopped
1/2 c. shredded Cheddar cheese
1/4 c. chow mein noodles

Cook egg noodles according to package directions; drain. Combine with remaining ingredients except chow mein noodles in an ungreased 11"x7" baking pan. Bake, uncovered, at 350 degrees for 25 minutes. Top with chow mein noodles and bake for an additional 10 minutes. Serves 4 to 6.

Jen Burnham
Delaware, OH

This is such an easy recipe...everything is mixed right in the baking pan.

Potato Puff Casserole

1 lb. ground beef
10-3/4 oz. can cream of
  mushroom soup
3 14-1/2 oz. cans green beans,
  drained
12 slices pasteurized process
  cheese spread
16-oz. pkg. frozen potato puffs

In a skillet over medium heat, brown beef; drain and stir in soup. Pour beef mixture into a greased 13"x9" baking pan. Top with green beans and sliced cheese. Arrange a single layer of potato puffs over cheese. Cover with aluminum foil and bake at 400 degrees for 20 minutes, or until cheese is melted. Uncover and bake again for 10 minutes, or until potato puffs are golden. Serves 6 to 8.

17

Dawn Henning
Gooseberry Patch

A family-favorite recipe that can be made in advance and frozen for a future hearty meal.

Blue-Ribbon Corn Dog Bake

1/3 c. sugar
1 egg, beaten
1 c. all-purpose flour
3/4 T. baking powder
1/2 t. salt
1/2 c. yellow cornmeal
1/2 T. butter, melted
3/4 c. milk
16-oz. pkg. hot dogs, sliced into
    bite-size pieces

In a small bowl, mix together sugar and egg. In a separate bowl, mix together flour, baking powder and salt. Add flour mixture to sugar mixture. Add cornmeal, butter and milk, stirring just to combine. Fold in hot dog pieces. Pour into a well-greased 8"x8" baking pan. Bake, uncovered, at 375 degrees for about 15 minutes, or until a toothpick inserted near the center comes out clean. Serves 6.

Tiffani Schulte
Wyandotte, MI
This casserole is oh-so easy
and it really does taste
like a county fair
corn dog!

Oodles of Noodles Chili Bake

12-oz. pkg. wide egg noodles,
    uncooked
1 lb. ground beef
14-1/2 oz. can diced tomatoes
15-oz. can corn, drained
15-oz. can chili
1 c. shredded Cheddar cheese,
    divided

Cook noodles according to package directions; drain and set aside. Meanwhile, brown beef in a skillet over medium heat; drain. Combine tomatoes with juice and remaining ingredients except 1/4 cup cheese in a lightly greased 13"x9" baking pan. Top with remaining cheese. Bake, uncovered, at 350 degrees for about 20 minutes, or until heated through. Serves 4.

Robin Kessler
Fresno, CA

Create a different dish by adding your favorite vegetables. It's foolproof and delicious either way!

Sloppy Joe Casserole

1 lb. ground beef
1 onion, diced
1 green pepper, diced
salt to taste
10-3/4 oz. can tomato soup
1/2 c. water
1 t. Worcestershire sauce
7-1/2 oz. tube refrigerated
   biscuits
1/2 c. shredded Cheddar cheese

Brown beef with onion, pepper and salt in a skillet over medium heat; drain. Stir in soup, water and Worcestershire sauce; heat to a boil. Spoon beef mixture into a greased 1-1/2 quart casserole dish. Arrange biscuits on top of beef mixture around the edges of the dish. Bake, uncovered, at 400 degrees for 15 minutes, or until biscuits are golden. Sprinkle cheese over biscuits; bake again for 15 minutes, or until cheese is melted. Serves 4.

Amy Hunt
Traphill, NC

This is a less messy way to eat a Sloppy Joe, but just as good.

Cowpoke Casserole

1 lb. ground beef
1/2 onion, chopped
salt and pepper to taste
1 t. chili powder
15-1/2 oz. can chili beans
8-oz. can tomato sauce
1/2 c. water
8-1/2 oz. pkg. cornbread mix
1/3 c. milk
1 egg, beaten

Brown beef with onion in an oven-proof skillet over medium heat. Drain; add salt and pepper to taste. Stir in chili powder, beans, tomato sauce and water. Simmer for 5 minutes; remove from heat. In a separate bowl, stir together cornbread mix, milk and egg; spoon over beef mixture and place skillet in oven. Bake, uncovered, at 350 degrees for 25 minutes, or until cornbread topping is golden and cooked through. Serves 4 to 6.

**Debbie Hutchinson
Spring, TX**

A cast-iron skillet is perfect for this dish... it can go right into the oven to bake!

Reuben Casserole

6 slices rye bread, cubed
16-oz. can sauerkraut, drained
   and rinsed
1 lb. sliced deli corned beef,
   cut into strips
3/4 c. Thousand Island salad
   dressing
2 c. shredded Swiss cheese

Arrange bread cubes in a greased
13"x9" baking pan; cover with
sauerkraut. Layer corned beef over
sauerkraut; drizzle salad dressing over
top. Cover with aluminum foil and
bake at 400 degrees for 20 minutes.
Remove foil; sprinkle with cheese
and bake, uncovered, for another
10 minutes, or until cheese is melted
and bubbly. Serves 6.

Jo Ann
An all-time favorite deli
sandwich turned into a quick
and simple casserole!

Mom's Texas Hash

1 lb. ground beef
2 onions, sliced
1 green pepper, chopped
1 c. stewed tomatoes
1/2 to 1 t. chili powder
1 t. salt

Brown beef, onions and green
pepper in a skillet over medium heat;
drain. Stir in tomatoes with juice and
seasonings. Cook over medium heat
until warmed through, about
8 minutes; spoon into an ungreased
one-quart casserole dish. Bake,
uncovered, at 350 degrees for
15 to 20 minutes. Serves 4.

Ginger O'Connell
Hazel Park, MI
Simply said...this is good!

Autumn Pork Chop Bake

14-1/2 oz. can cream of celery
    soup
1-1/2 c. herb-flavored stuffing
    mix
1/2 c. corn
1/4 c. celery, chopped
4 boneless pork chops
1 t. brown sugar, packed
1 t. spicy brown mustard

In a bowl, combine soup, stuffing
mix, corn and celery. Spoon into a
greased 9" pie plate. Top with pork
chops. In a bowl, mix together
brown sugar and mustard; spoon
over pork chops. Bake, uncovered, at
400 degrees for 30 minutes, or until
hot and pork chops are cooked
through. Serves 4.

Elizabeth Gilvin
Lexington, KY
This is one of my family's
favorite recipes on
a cold day!

Company Breakfast Casserole

1/2 lb. bacon
1/2 c. onion, chopped
1 doz. eggs, beaten
1 c. milk
16-oz. pkg. frozen shredded
    hashbrowns, thawed
1-1/2 c. shredded sharp Cheddar
    cheese
1 t. salt
1/2 t. pepper

In a skillet over medium heat, cook bacon until crisp. Crumble and set aside, reserving 2 tablespoons drippings. Sauté onion in reserved drippings until tender; set aside. In a bowl, beat eggs and milk; stir in onion, bacon and remaining ingredients. Pour into a greased 13"x9" baking pan. Bake, uncovered, at 350 degrees for 40 to 45 minutes, until a knife inserted near the middle comes out clean. Serves 6.

25

Vickie Tiche
Lincoln, CA

This hearty breakfast casserole is perfect to serve to overnight guests anytime.

Baked Stuffed Tomatoes

4 tomatoes
1/2 c. dry bread crumbs
2 t. butter, melted
1 t. grated Parmesan cheese
1/2 t. dried basil
1/2 t. dried oregano
2 t. fresh parsley, finely chopped
salt and pepper to taste

Slice tops off tomatoes; set aside.
Scoop out some of the pulp from
tomatoes; discard. Blend together
remaining ingredients. Spoon crumb
mixture evenly into each tomato,
pressing firmly. Place tomatoes in
a greased 9"x9" baking pan. Bake,
uncovered, at 350 degrees for
20 minutes, or until topping is
golden. Makes 4 servings.

Donna Dye
London, OH
Rediscover this old-fashioned
favorite...it's as good
as ever!

Mexican Lasagna

1 lb. ground beef
1-1/4 oz. pkg. taco seasoning
8-oz. pkg. 10-inch flour tortillas
8-oz. pkg. cream cheese,
    softened and divided
1 c. shredded Cheddar cheese,
    divided
8-oz. can tomato sauce, divided

Brown beef in a skillet over medium heat; drain. Add taco seasoning and cook according to package directions. Spread 2 tortillas with 1/4 of the cream cheese and place cheese-side up in an ungreased 13"x9" baking pan; spoon 1/4 of the beef mixture over tortillas. Top with 1/4 the shredded cheese and 1/4 the tomato sauce. Repeat layers 3 more times, ending with cheese. Bake, uncovered, at 350 degrees for about 25 minutes, or until heated through and cheese is melted. Serves 4 to 6.

Amanda Melancon
Hahira, GA

My daughter and I love
this...plus we always
have all the ingredients
on hand!

Cheeseburger Bake

8-oz. tube refrigerated crescent
  rolls
1 lb. ground beef
1-1/4 oz. pkg. taco seasoning
15-oz. can tomato sauce
2 c. shredded Cheddar cheese

Unroll crescent roll dough; press
into a greased 9" round baking pan,
pinching seams closed. Bake at
350 degrees for 10 minutes; set aside.
Meanwhile, brown beef in a skillet
over medium heat; drain. Add taco
seasoning and sauce; heat through.
Spoon over crescent rolls and
sprinkle cheese on top. Bake,
uncovered, for 10 to 15 minutes.
Let stand 5 minutes before serving.
Serves 4.

Jennifer Williams
Los Angeles, CA
This hearty meal is great
after a long day of work
and errands...so filling.

Crescent Roll Lasagna

1-1/2 lbs. ground beef
1 onion, diced
salt and pepper to taste
15-oz. can tomato sauce
1 T. Worcestershire sauce
1/2 t. garlic salt
1 t. Italian seasoning, divided
2 T. brown sugar, packed
2 c. shredded Cheddar cheese
2 c. shredded mozzarella cheese
2 8-oz. tubes refrigerated
    crescent rolls
8-oz. container sour cream

In a skillet over medium heat, brown
beef, onion, salt and pepper; drain.
Add sauces, garlic salt, 1/2 teaspoon
Italian seasoning and brown sugar.
Transfer to a greased 13"x9" baking
pan. Top with cheeses. Unroll
crescent rolls; spread with about a
tablespoon of sour cream and
sprinkle with remaining Italian
seasoning. Roll up crescent rolls;
place on top of cheese. Bake,
uncovered, at 350 degrees for 35 to
40 minutes, until bubbly and rolls
are golden. Serves 6 to 8.

Faith Bedard
Hallock, MN
A family favorite...it's
so good!

29

Eggplant Casserole

1 lb. ground beef
1 onion, diced
salt, pepper and garlic powder
   to taste
1 eggplant, quartered
2 eggs, beaten
2 T. grated Parmesan cheese
10 saltine crackers, crushed
2 T. butter, sliced

Brown beef and onion with salt, pepper and garlic powder in a skillet over medium heat; drain. Meanwhile, in a saucepan, cover eggplant with water; boil until tender. Scoop cooked eggplant out of its skin; let cool. Discard skin. Combine beef mixture, eggplant, eggs and Parmesan in a greased 13"x9" baking pan, mixing well. Top with crackers and dot with butter. Bake, uncovered, at 325 degrees for 30 minutes, or until heated through. Serves 6 to 8.

Gina Robinson
Streetman, TX

This recipe was a favorite when I was growing up. It has been passed on for generations.

Mexican Cornbread Bake

1 lb. ground beef
4-1/2 oz. can chopped green
  chiles
1 onion, chopped
2 t. Mexican seasoning
1 T. chili powder
8-oz. can Mexican-style tomato
  sauce
8-1/2 oz. pkg. cornbread mix

Brown beef in a skillet over medium heat; drain. Add chiles, onion and seasonings; cook until onion is tender. Add tomato sauce and simmer. Prepare cornbread mix according to package directions; pour half the batter into a greased 2-quart casserole dish. Spoon beef mixture over batter; top with remaining batter. Bake, uncovered, at 350 degrees for 25 to 30 minutes, until golden. Serves 4 to 6.

Terri Taylor
Jonesville, LA

Spicy beef tucked between layers of golden cornbread...yum!

Brock's Pimento & Cheese Grits Casserole

3 c. quick-cooking grits,
  uncooked
1/2 c. butter
1/2 c. whipping cream
1 t. salt
16-oz. pkg. shredded Cheddar
  cheese
4-oz. jar diced pimentos,
  drained
1 c. mayonnaise
8-oz. pkg. cream cheese,
  softened
2 t. pepper
1/2 c. green onions, chopped

Cook grits according to package directions. In a bowl, combine grits, butter, cream and salt. In a separate bowl, combine remaining ingredients except onions; mix well. Combine the 2 mixtures; stir together. Pour into a greased 13"x9" baking pan. Bake, uncovered, at 375 degrees for 35 to 40 minutes, until bubbly. Top with onions. Serves 8.

Brock Rogers
Louisville, MS
This is a different spin on traditional Southern cheese grits.

Harvest Casserole

1/2 c. long-cooking rice,
  uncooked
4 redskin potatoes, cut into
  thin wedges
1/4 c. butter, sliced and divided
1 T. fresh sage, chopped
3 red peppers, chopped
1 onion, sliced
2 zucchini, thinly sliced
1 c. shredded Cheddar cheese

Cook rice according to package directions; set aside. Place potatoes in a greased 2-1/2 quart casserole dish. Dot with half the butter; layer half the sage, peppers, onion, zucchini and rice. Layer ingredients again; cover with aluminum foil. Bake at 350 degrees for one hour, or until potatoes are tender. Remove foil; sprinkle cheese over top and return to oven until cheese is melted. Serves 6.

33

Regina Wickline
Pebble Beach, CA

This casserole is packed full of wonderful vegetables grown in your own backyard or from the nearest farmers' market.

Hearty Stuffed Pepper Casserole

2-1/2 c. herb-flavored stuffing
   mix, divided
1 T. butter, melted
1 lb. ground beef
1/2 c. onion, chopped
14-1/2 oz. can whole tomatoes,
   chopped
8-oz. can corn, drained
salt and pepper to taste
2 green peppers, quartered

Mix together 1/4 cup dry stuffing
mix and butter; set aside. Brown
beef and onion in a skillet over
medium-high heat; drain. Stir in
tomatoes, corn, salt and pepper;
add remaining stuffing mix. Arrange
green peppers in an ungreased
2-quart casserole dish; spoon beef
mixture over top. Cover and bake
at 400 degrees for 25 minutes.
Sprinkle with reserved stuffing
mixture. Bake, uncovered, for
5 additional minutes, or until
peppers are tender. Serves 4 to 6.

Vickie
Love stuffed peppers? Try
this casserole version for
a new family favorite!

Taco-Filled Pasta Shells

2 lbs. ground beef
2 1-1/4 oz. pkgs. taco seasoning
8-oz. pkg. cream cheese, cubed
2 12-oz. pkgs. jumbo pasta
   shells, uncooked
1/4 c. butter, melted
1 c. salsa
1 c. taco sauce
1 c. shredded Cheddar cheese
1 c. shredded Monterey Jack
   cheese
1-1/2 c. tortilla chips, crushed
Optional: sour cream, chopped
   green onions

Brown beef in a skillet over medium heat; drain. Add taco seasoning and cook according to package directions. Add cream cheese; stir to melt. Remove beef mixture to a bowl and chill for one hour. Meanwhile, cook pasta shells according to package directions; drain. Toss shells with butter. Fill each shell with 3 tablespoons of beef mixture. Spoon salsa into a greased 13"x9" baking pan; place shells on top of salsa and cover with taco sauce. Bake, covered, for 30 minutes. Uncover, sprinkle with cheeses and tortilla chips. Bake for 15 minutes, or until heated through. Serves 4 to 6.

Brittany Cornelius
Chambersburg, PA

A Mexican twist on an Italian dish...my whole family loves this!

Maggie's Kickin' King Ranch Chicken

5 to 6 boneless, skinless chicken
   breasts, cooked and cubed
2 10-3/4 oz. cans cream of
   chicken soup
2 10-3/4 oz. cans cream of
   mushroom soup
2 10-oz. cans diced tomatoes
   with green chiles
1 T. chili powder
2 t. garlic salt
1-1/3 c. water
salt and pepper to taste
2 18-oz. pkgs. restaurant-style
   tortilla chips, divided
2 12-oz. pkgs. shredded
   Cheddar cheese

In a large bowl, combine chicken and
remaining ingredients except chips
and cheese; mix well. Place chips in a
single layer in the bottom and up the
sides of an ungreased 15"x10" baking
pan; reserve any remaining chips.
Spoon chicken mixture over chips.
Cover with cheese. Bake, uncovered,
at 350 degrees for 30 minutes, or
until bubbly. Serve with remaining
chips. Serves 8 to 10.

Maggie Jo Tucker
Hartsfield, GA
I got this recipe from
my dear friend Aunt B,
but I have adapted it
to fit our tastes!

Chicken-Broccoli Divan

2 c. cooked chicken, cubed
16-oz. pkg. frozen broccoli
 flowerets, thawed
2 10-3/4 oz. cans cream of
 chicken soup
3/4 c. mayonnaise
1 t. lemon juice
1/2 c. shredded Cheddar cheese

Place chicken in a greased 13"x9" baking pan. Layer broccoli on top. In a bowl, stir together soup, mayonnaise and lemon juice. Pour soup mixture over broccoli; top with cheese. Bake, uncovered, at 350 degrees for 45 minutes, or until bubbly. Serves 4.

37

Tiffany Mayberry
Harriman, TN

This is a delightful recipe I remember my mother cooking for me when I was a little girl.

Green Bean, Ham & Potato Bake

1 onion, chopped
2 cloves garlic, minced
1 T. butter
3 potatoes, diced
salt and pepper to taste
2 14-1/2 oz. cans green beans,
    drained
1-1/2 c. cooked ham, cubed
2 sprigs fresh rosemary, chopped
1 c. water

In a skillet over medium-high heat, sauté onion and garlic in butter; add potatoes, salt and pepper. Cook until potatoes are crisp. In a greased 13"x9" baking pan, combine potato mixture, green beans, ham and rosemary. Drizzle water over all. Cover with aluminum foil and bake at 350 degrees for one hour, or until potatoes are tender. Serves 6.

Rachel Kowasic
Connellsville, PA
I grew up watching my stepmom make this tasty recipe with fresh green beans from her garden.

Easy Cheesy Ratatouille

1 eggplant, peeled and cut into
   1-inch cubes
1 onion, diced
1 red pepper, diced
1 zucchini, cut into 1-inch cubes
1/4 c. sun-dried tomato
   vinaigrette
14-1/2 oz. can diced tomatoes
1/4 c. grated Parmesan cheese
1 c. shredded mozzarella cheese

Sauté vegetables with vinaigrette
in a large oven-safe skillet over
medium heat. Add tomatoes with
juice; cook for 15 minutes. Sprinkle
with cheeses. Bake, uncovered, at
350 degrees for 15 minutes, or until
vegetables are tender. Serves 6 to 8.

39

Amy Butcher
Columbus, GA

When I first had this at a
church potluck, I made sure
to go back for seconds and
to ask for the recipe!

Johnny Marzetti

2 T. oil
1 onion, chopped
1 green pepper, chopped
1 lb. ground beef
28-oz. jar spaghetti sauce
1-1/2 c. elbow macaroni, cooked
2 c. shredded Cheddar cheese

Heat oil in a skillet. Add onion and
green pepper; sauté until softened.
Add beef and cook until browned;
drain. Stir in spaghetti sauce and
macaroni; pour into an ungreased
13"x9" baking pan. Sprinkle
with cheese. Bake, uncovered,
at 350 degrees for one hour.
Serves 4 to 6.

Linda Karner
Pisgah Forest, NC

No one knows about
this dish's mysterious
name...but everyone
agrees it tastes incredible!

Zucchini Boats

1 lb. ground beef
1 onion, chopped
16-oz. jar spaghetti sauce
2 large zucchini, halved
   lengthwise
salt and pepper to taste
1/2 c. grated parmesan cheese
1 c. shredded mozzarella cheese

Brown beef and onion in a skillet over medium heat; drain. Add spaghetti sauce to beef mixture and stir until combined. Meanwhile, lay zucchini halves, cut-side down, on a microwave-safe plate. Cook on high setting until fork-tender, about 5 to 10 minutes. Scoop out seeds and some surrounding pulp; discard. Sprinkle zucchini halves with salt and pepper; place in a greased 13"x9" baking pan. Spoon beef mixture into hollowed-out zucchini halves and top with cheeses. Bake, uncovered, at 350 degrees for about 40 minutes, or until heated through and cheese is bubbly. Serves 4.

Audrey Piatti
Leonardo, NJ

I came up with this recipe because I could never decide what to do with all my zucchini...who knew these would be so good?

Buffalo Chicken Quinoa Casserole

1 c. quinoa, uncooked
3 c. shredded Cheddar cheese,
   divided
1 c. buffalo wing sauce, divided
1 c. sour cream
1/4 c. butter, softened
1/4 c. milk
1/2 t. garlic salt
1/4 t. pepper
1 t. dried basil
4 boneless, skinless chicken
   breasts, cooked and cubed

Cook quinoa according to package directions. Meanwhile, in a large bowl, combine 2 cups cheese and 1/2 cup buffalo wing sauce with remaining ingredients except chicken and quinoa. Fold in quinoa. Spread mixture into a greased 13"x9" baking pan. Top with chicken. Drizzle with remaining buffalo wing sauce and sprinkle with remaining cheese. Bake, covered, at 350 degrees for 45 minutes, or until heated through and bubbly. Serves 8.

Trish McGregor
Prospect, VA

Forged out of my family's love of buffalo chicken...this casserole has become a favorite!

Cheesy Baked Tortellini

10-oz. pkg. refrigerated cheese
  tortellini
2 c. marinara sauce
1/3 c. mascarpone cheese or
  softened cream cheese
1/4 c. fresh Italian parsley,
  chopped
2 t. fresh thyme, chopped
5 slices smoked mozzarella cheese
1/4 c. shredded Parmesan cheese

Prepare tortellini according to package directions; drain and set aside. Meanwhile, in a bowl, combine marinara sauce, mascarpone or cream cheese, parsley and thyme. Fold in tortellini. Transfer to a greased 9"x9" baking pan. Top with mozzarella and Parmesan cheeses. Bake, covered, at 350 degrees for about 30 minutes, or until cheese is melted and sauce is bubbly. Serves 4 to 6.

43

Pat Wissler
Harrisburg, PA

When I make this hearty dish, I usually double the recipe and freeze some for later... very convenient!

Cheesy Sausage-Potato Casserole

3 to 4 potatoes, sliced
1 lb. smoked sausage, sliced
1 onion, chopped
1/2 c. butter, sliced
1 c. shredded Cheddar cheese

Layer potatoes, sausage and onion in a 13"x9" baking pan sprayed with non-stick vegetable spray. Dot with butter; sprinkle with cheese. Bake, uncovered, at 350 degrees for 1-1/2 hours, or until potatoes are tender. Serves 6 to 8.

J.J. Presley
Portland, TX

Add some fresh green beans too if you like.

Crab & Shrimp Casserole

2 8-oz. cans crabmeat, drained
2 4-oz. cans tiny shrimp,
   drained
2 c. celery, chopped
1 green pepper, chopped
1 onion, chopped
1 T. Worcestershire sauce
1 t. sugar
1 c. mayonnaise
salt and pepper to taste
1 c. soft bread crumbs, buttered
2 T. lemon juice
Garnish: thin lemon slices

Mix together all ingredients except
bread crumbs, lemon juice and
garnish. Place in a greased
13"x9" baking pan. Spread bread
crumbs over crab mixture. Bake,
uncovered, at 350 degrees for
30 to 45 minutes, until heated
through. Sprinkle lemon juice over
casserole. Garnish with lemon slices.
Serves 4 to 6.

45

Jennie Gist
Gooseberry Patch

The yummy taste of
the sea in a
convenient casserole!

Beef Burgundy

1-1/2 lb. beef sirloin, cubed
2 1-1/2 oz. pkgs. onion soup mix
2 10-3/4 oz. cans cream of
    mushroom soup
1/2 c. burgundy wine or beef
    broth
1/2 c. water
cooked rice or egg noodles

Combine all ingredients except
rice or noodles in a Dutch oven.
Bake, covered, at 325 degrees for
2-1/2 hours, or until bubbly and
beef is cooked through. Serve beef
mixture over rice or noodles. Makes
6 to 8 servings.

Melia Himich
Manchester, MI
An easy-to-prepare dish
that's delicious served
over noodles or rice.

Meatball Sub Casserole

1 loaf Italian bread, cut into
    1-inch thick slices
8-oz. pkg. cream cheese,
    softened
1/2 c. mayonnaise
1 t. Italian seasoning
1/4 t. pepper
2 c. shredded mozzarella cheese,
    divided
1-lb. pkg. frozen meatballs,
    thawed
28-oz. jar pasta sauce
1 c. water

Arrange bread slices in a single layer
in an ungreased 13"x9" baking pan;
set aside. In a bowl, combine cream
cheese, mayonnaise and seasonings;
spread over bread slices. Sprinkle
with 1/2 cup cheese; set aside. Gently
mix together meatballs, spaghetti
sauce and water; spoon over cheese.
Sprinkle with remaining cheese.
Bake, uncovered, at 350 degrees for
30 minutes. Serves 4.

Christi Wroe
Bedford, PA
Serve this tasty casserole
with a green salad and
garlic bread...delicious!

Eggplant Parmesan

4 eggs, beaten
3 T. water
2 eggplants, peeled and sliced
   1/4-inch thick
2 c. Italian-style dry bread
   crumbs
1-1/2 c. grated Parmesan cheese,
   divided
28-oz. jar garden-style pasta
   sauce, divided
1-1/2 c. shredded mozzarella
   cheese

Whisk together eggs and water in a shallow bowl. Dip eggplant slices into egg mixture. Arrange slices in a single layer on a greased baking sheet; bake at 350 degrees for 25 minutes, or until tender. Set aside. Mix bread crumbs and 1/2 cup Parmesan cheese; set aside. Spread a small amount of sauce in an ungreased 13"x9" baking pan; layer half the eggplant, one cup sauce and one cup crumb mixture. Repeat layering. Cover with aluminum foil and bake for 45 minutes. Remove foil; sprinkle with mozzarella cheese. Bake, uncovered, for an additional 10 minutes. Serves 6 to 8.

Tammy Dillow
Raceland, KY

For me, this is a down-home dish that's great to enjoy with family & friends, no matter what the occasion.

Sausage & Chicken Cassoulet

1 lb. hot Italian ground pork
    sausage
1 c. carrot, peeled and thinly
    sliced
1 onion, diced
2 t. garlic, minced
1 c. red wine or beef broth
2 T. tomato paste
1 bay leaf
1 t. dried thyme
1 t. dried rosemary
salt and pepper to taste
2 c. cooked chicken, diced
2 15-oz. cans Great Northern
    beans

Brown sausage in an oven-safe Dutch
oven over medium heat; drain. Add
carrot, onion and garlic. Sauté for
3 minutes. Add wine or broth,
tomato paste and seasonings; bring
to a boil. Remove from heat; stir in
chicken and beans with liquid. Bake,
covered, at 350 degrees for
45 minutes, or until bubbly. Discard
bay leaf before serving. Serves 4 to 6.

Diane Stout
Zeeland, MI

This savory casserole is
full of wonderful flavors...
better bring along some
recipe cards to share!

49

Polenta Casserole

3 c. water
1 t. salt
1 c. yellow cornmeal
1/2 t. Montreal steak seasoning
1 c. shredded sharp Cheddar
  cheese, divided
1 lb. ground beef
1 c. onion, chopped
1 zucchini, halved lengthwise and
  sliced
1 T. olive oil
2 14-1/2 oz. cans diced tomatoes,
  drained
6-oz. can tomato paste
Garnish: fresh parsley, chopped

In a 2-quart saucepan, bring water
and salt to a boil. Whisk in cornmeal;
reduce heat to low. Simmer, whisking
constantly, for 3 minutes, or until
thickened. Remove from heat; stir in
steak seasoning and 1/4 cup cheese.
Spread cornmeal mixture into a
greased 11"x7" baking pan. Brown
beef with onion and zucchini in oil
in a skillet over medium-high heat;
drain. Stir in tomatoes and tomato
paste; simmer for 10 minutes, stirring
often. Spoon beef mixture over
cornmeal mixture; sprinkle with
remaining cheese. Bake, uncovered,
at 350 degrees for 30 minutes, or
until bubbly. Garnish with parsley.
Serves 6.

Gail Blain Prather
Hastings, NE

Easy, filling and
best of all, yummy!

Mom's Chicken Casserole

6-oz. pkg. rice pilaf mix
4 to 6 boneless, skinless chicken
   breasts
2 c. stewed tomatoes

Prepare rice pilaf according to package directions, cooking for just half the time. Transfer pilaf to a greased 13"x9" baking pan. Place chicken breasts over pilaf. Spoon tomatoes over chicken. Bake, covered with aluminum foil, at 350 degrees for one hour, or until chicken juices run clear and all liquid is absorbed. Serves 4 to 6.

51

Samantha Fishkin
Lauderdale Lakes, FL
This meal is very easy to create, uses very few ingredients and is delicious!

Daddy's Shepherd's Pie

1 lb. ground beef
10-3/4 oz. can cream of
   mushroom soup
2/3 c. water
7.2-oz. pkg. homestyle creamy
   butter-flavored instant mashed
   potato flakes
2 c. corn
8-oz. pkg. shredded Cheddar
   cheese

Brown beef in a skillet over medium heat; drain. Stir in soup and water; simmer until heated through. Meanwhile, prepare potato flakes as package directs; set aside. Place beef mixture in a 13"x9" baking pan sprayed with non-stick vegetable spray. Top with corn; spread potatoes evenly across top. Sprinkle with cheese. Bake, uncovered, at 425 degrees for about 10 minutes, or until hot and cheese is melted. Makes 6 to 8 servings.

Sheila Wakeman
Winnsboro, TX
I can remember going to Dad's house on the weekends, and we would make this dish together.

Hobo Dinner

1-1/2 lbs. ground beef
1 t. Worcestershire sauce
1/2 t. seasoned pepper
1/8 t. garlic powder
3 redskin potatoes, sliced
1 onion, sliced
3 carrots, peeled and sliced
olive oil and dried parsley
    to taste

In a bowl, combine beef, Worcestershire sauce, pepper and garlic powder; form into 4 to 6 patties. Place each patty on an 18-inch length of aluminum foil. Divide slices of potato, onion and carrots evenly and place on top of each patty. Sprinkle with olive oil and parsley to taste. Wrap tightly in aluminum foil and arrange packets on a baking sheet. Bake at 375 degrees for one hour, or until vegetables are tender and beef is cooked through. Serves 4 to 6.

53

Denise Piccirilli
Huber Heights, OH

My mom and I have made this recipe for years. It's quick, delicious and so easy the kids can help assemble it.

Baked Chicken Chow Mein

10-3/4 oz. can cream of chicken soup
10-3/4 oz. can cream of celery soup
5-oz. can evaporated milk
4-oz. can mushroom stems and pieces, drained
8-oz. can water chestnuts, drained and chopped
2 c. cooked chicken, cubed
5-oz. can chow mein noodles, divided
2 t. Worcestershire sauce
1 to 2 t. curry powder
2 T. butter

In a bowl, combine soups and milk; fold in mushrooms, water chestnuts, chicken and half the chow mein noodles. Sprinkle with Worcestershire sauce and curry powder; stir to combine. Spread into a greased 2-quart casserole dish. Top with remaining noodles; dot with butter. Bake, uncovered, at 350 degrees for 30 minutes, or until bubbly. Serves 4 to 6.

Judi Leaming
Dover, DE

Our daughter, Ami, earned a 4-H Blue Ribbon for this dish!

Hunter's Pie

1 lb. roast beef, cooked and
   cubed
12-oz. jar beef gravy
8-oz. can sliced carrots, drained
8-oz. can green beans, drained
9-inch deep-dish pie crust,
   baked
11-oz. tube refrigerated bread
   sticks

Combine all ingredients except pie
crust and bread sticks; spread into
pie crust. Arrange unbaked bread
sticks on top, criss-cross style. Bake
at 350 degrees for 20 minutes, or
until heated through and bread sticks
are golden. Serves 4.

55

Heidi Maurer
Garrett, IN

My 3-year-old son Hunter
loves this and my 8-year-old
son Luke does too...but
without the beans!

Shipwreck Casserole

1 lb. lean ground beef
1/4 t. salt
1/4 t. pepper
4 potatoes, peeled and sliced
1 onion, chopped
8-oz. can pork & beans
10-3/4 oz. can tomato soup

In a skillet over medium heat, brown beef with salt and pepper; drain and set aside. Place potatoes in a greased 2-quart casserole dish; top with onion. Cover with beef mixture. Spoon pork & beans over beef, then pour tomato soup over all. Bake, covered, at 375 degrees for one hour, or until potatoes are tender and casserole is bubbly. Serves 6 to 8.

Janis Parr
Ontario, Canada

The kids come running to the table whenever I make Shipwreck Casserole!

Ham & Cheese Spaghetti

1 lb. cooked ham, cubed
1 to 2 t. olive oil
1 green pepper, diced
1 onion, diced
2 to 3 cloves garlic, pressed
15-oz. can tomato sauce
14-1/2 oz. can diced tomatoes
Italian seasoning to taste
16-oz. pkg. spaghetti, uncooked
16-oz. pkg. sliced American
  cheese

In a skillet over medium heat, lightly brown ham in oil. Add pepper and onion; sauté until tender. Stir in garlic, tomato sauce, tomatoes with juice and seasoning; bring to a boil. Reduce heat; cover and simmer for 20 to 30 minutes, stirring occasionally. Meanwhile, cook spaghetti according to package directions; drain. In a greased 13"x9" baking pan, place a layer of spaghetti, a layer of ham mixture and 3 to 4 cheese slices. Repeat layering 2 to 3 times, ending with sauce and cheese. Bake, uncovered, at 375 degrees for about 10 minutes, or until hot and bubbly. Serves 4 to 6.

Cynthia Besse
Midlothian, TX

This family favorite dates back to the Depression and has been a regular at our family table ever since.

Sweet Corn & Rice Casserole

2 T. butter
1 green pepper, chopped
1 onion, chopped
15-1/2 oz. can creamed corn
11-oz. can sweet corn & diced
   peppers, drained
11-oz. can corn, drained
6 c. cooked rice
10-oz. can diced tomatoes with
   green chiles, drained
8-oz. pkg. mild Mexican
   pasteurized process cheese
   spread, cubed
1/2 t. salt
1/4 t. pepper
1/2 c. shredded Cheddar cheese

Melt butter in a large skillet over medium heat. Add green pepper and onion; sauté 5 minutes, or until tender. Stir in remaining ingredients except shredded cheese; spoon into a lightly greased 13"x9" baking pan. Bake, uncovered, at 350 degrees for 25 to 30 minutes, until heated through. Top with shredded cheese; bake an additional 5 minutes, until cheese melts. Makes 10 to 12 servings.

Linda Stone
Algood, TN

Roll up leftovers in a flour tortilla for a hearty snack.

Baked Chicken Jambalaya

1 lb. pkg. smoked beef sausage,
   sliced
1/4 c. butter
4 c. cooked chicken, cubed
16-oz. pkg. frozen mixed
   vegetables, thawed
1 onion, sliced
4 stalks celery, sliced
1 green pepper, thinly sliced
2 c. shredded mozzarella or
   Cheddar cheese
16-oz. pkg. bowtie pasta,
   cooked

In a skillet over medium-high heat,
sauté sausage in butter until
browned. Add chicken to skillet with
sausage. Transfer sausage mixture
into a 13"x9" baking pan; add mixed
vegetables, onion, celery and green
pepper. Top with cheese and cover
with aluminum foil. Bake at
350 degrees for about 30 minutes,
or until veggies are crisp-tender and
cheese is melted. Serve over pasta.
Serves 8.

59

Vicki Holland
Hampton, GA
I came up with this dish on
short notice to feed a bunch
of hungry teenagers with
what I had on hand. I was
surprised at the great
blend of flavors.

Hamburger Stroganoff Casserole

16-oz. pkg. wide egg noodles,
   uncooked
2 lbs. ground beef
l onion, chopped
10-3/4 oz. can low-fat cream
   of mushroom soup
8-oz. container sour cream
salt and pepper to taste

Cook noodles according to package directions; drain. Meanwhile, brown beef and onion in a large skillet over medium heat; drain. Mix soup and sour cream into beef mixture; add noodles. Season with salt and pepper. Spoon into a lightly greased 13"x9" baking pan. Bake, uncovered, at 350 degrees for 30 minutes, or until heated through. Serves 8 to 10.

Pamela Berry
Huntington, IN

This casserole is a huge hit whenever I put it on the table!

Apple-Pork Chop Casserole

1 T. oil
8 boneless pork chops
2 6-oz. pkgs. herb-flavored
   stuffing mix
2 21-oz. cans apple pie filling

Heat oil in a skillet over medium-high heat. Cook pork chops in oil until both sides are browned. Meanwhile, prepare stuffing according to package directions. Pour pie filling into a lightly greased 13"x9" baking pan; lay pork chops on top. Cover with stuffing. Bake, uncovered, at 325 degrees for 45 minutes to one hour, until pork chops are cooked through. Serves 8.

Gayla Reyes
Hamilton, OH
One of my family's favorites. It's so quick and easy.

Chicken & Asparagus Bake

6 boneless, skinless chicken
   breasts, cooked and cubed
3 14-1/2 oz. cans asparagus
   pieces, drained
2-oz. jar chopped pimentos,
   drained
3/4 c. slivered almonds
3 10-3/4 oz. cans cream of
   mushroom soup
2 2.8-oz. cans French fried
   onions

Layer chicken, asparagus, pimentos,
almonds and soup in a lightly greased
2-1/2 quart casserole dish. Cover with
aluminum foil; bake at 350 degrees
for 30 to 40 minutes, until bubbly.
Uncover and top with onions. Bake
for an additional 5 minutes. Serves
6 to 8.

Marilyn Morel
Keene, NH

A delicious casserole that's
simple to prepare and bakes
in under 45 minutes!

Hearty Breakfast Casserole

6 to 8 bread slices
3-oz. pkg. ready-to-use bacon
   crumbles
1 lb. cooked ham, diced, or
   ground pork sausage, browned
2 c. shredded Cheddar cheese
10 eggs, beaten
1 c. milk
1 t. salt
1 t. pepper

Arrange bread slices in a single layer in a greased 13"x9" baking pan; top with bacon and ham or sausage. Sprinkle with cheese. Whisk together remaining ingredients. Pour egg mixture over top. Cover with aluminum foil and refrigerate overnight. Bake, covered, at 350 degrees for 45 minutes to one hour, until center is set. Serves 12.

63

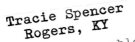

Tracie Spencer
Rogers, KY

An easy-to-assemble make-ahead breakfast... perfect for busy mornings or when you have brunch guests!

Broccoli Supreme

1 egg, beaten
10-oz. pkg. frozen chopped
    broccoli, partially thawed
    and drained
8-1/2 oz. can creamed corn
1 T. onion, grated
1/4 t. salt
1/8 t. pepper
1 c. herb-flavored stuffing mix
3 T. butter, melted

In a bowl, combine egg, broccoli,
corn, onion, salt and pepper. In a
separate bowl, toss stuffing mix
with butter. Stir 3/4 cup of stuffing
mixture into egg mixture. Turn into
an ungreased 8"x8" baking pan.
Sprinkle with remaining stuffing
mixture. Bake, uncovered, at
350 degrees for 35 to 40 minutes,
until bubbly. Makes 6 to 8 servings.

Linda Belon
Wintersville, OH
A delicious side that
whips up in a jiffy!

Family-Favorite Corn Soufflé

15-oz. can corn, drained
8-1/2 oz. pkg. cornbread mix
14-3/4 oz. can creamed corn
1 c. sour cream
1/4 c. butter, melted
8-oz. pkg. shredded Cheddar
   cheese

Combine all ingredients except cheese. Pour into a lightly greased 13"x9" baking pan. Cover with aluminum foil. Bake at 350 degrees for 30 minutes. Uncover; top with cheese. Return to oven and continue baking until cheese is bubbly and golden, about 15 minutes. Serves 8 to 10.

Donna Maltman
Toledo, OH

An absolute must-have for Thanksgiving dinner.

Italian Pie

1 lb. ground beef
garlic salt and pepper to taste
16-oz. jar spaghetti sauce
2 8-oz. cans refrigerated
   crescent rolls
1/2 c. shredded mozzarella cheese
1/2 c. shredded Colby cheese

Season beef with garlic salt and pepper to taste; brown in a skillet over medium heat. Drain; add spaghetti sauce to beef and simmer for 5 minutes. Layer one can of crescent rolls in the bottom of a greased 13"x9" baking dish; spread rolls to edges of pan. Spoon beef mixture over rolls; layer cheeses on top. Spread remaining can of crescent rolls over cheese layer; cover with aluminum foil. Bake at 350 degrees for 30 minutes. Remove foil and bake 15 more minutes, or until golden. Makes 12 servings.

Becky Hawkins
Spearfish, SD
Serve with a crisp Caesar salad for a complete meal.

Curry Chicken Casserole

1 c. long-cooking rice, uncooked
14-1/2 oz. can French-cut green
   beans, drained and divided
3 c. cooked chicken, chopped
8-oz. can sliced water chestnuts,
   drained
10-3/4 oz. can cream of chicken
   soup
1/4 c. chicken broth
1 c. mayonnaise
1 t. curry powder
1 c. French fried onions

Cook rice according to package
directions. Combine rice, half the
beans and remaining ingredients
except onions in a greased
13"x9" baking pan; mix well. Top
with remaining beans. Bake,
uncovered, at 350 degrees for
25 minutes, or until bubbling.
Sprinkle onions over top and bake
for another 5 minutes. Serves 6.

Jodi Griggs
Richmond, KY
My mother-in-law makes this
casserole for Sunday dinner,
and we all love it!

Seafood Enchiladas

3 c. chicken broth
1/3 c. all-purpose flour
14-1/2 oz. can diced tomatoes
3 green chiles, chopped
1/2 c. onion, chopped
1/2 t. garlic, minced
1 t. sugar
1 t. ground cumin
1/2 t. dried basil
1/2 t. dried oregano
salt and pepper to taste
1 lb. crabmeat
1/2 lb. cooked shrimp
12-oz. pkg. shredded Monterey
   Jack cheese
12 10-inch flour tortillas
3/4 c. sour cream

Combine broth with flour in a saucepan. Cook over medium heat until thickened, stirring constantly. Add tomatoes with juice, chiles, onion, garlic, sugar and seasonings. Bring to a simmer, stirring frequently. Remove from heat. Divide seafood and half of cheese evenly among tortillas; roll up and arrange seam-side down in a greased 15"x10" baking pan. Blend sour cream into tomato mixture. Spoon tomato mixture over enchiladas; sprinkle with remaining cheese. Bake, uncovered, at 400 degrees for 15 minutes, or until cheese melts. Serves 12.

Stephanie Monroe
Franklin, TN

These are great topped with some thick and chunky salsa plus a dollop of sour cream!

Alabama Chicken Casserole

2 to 3 c. cooked chicken,
    chopped
4 eggs, hard-boiled, peeled
    and chopped
2 c. cooked rice
1-1/2 c. celery, chopped
1 onion, chopped
2 10-3/4 oz. cans cream of
    mushroom soup
1 c. mayonnaise
2 T. lemon juice
3-oz. pkg. slivered almonds
5-oz. can chow mein noodles

Mix all ingredients except noodles in a large bowl. Transfer to a greased 13"x9" baking pan. Cover and refrigerate overnight. Uncover and bake at 350 degrees for one hour, or until hot and bubbly. Top with noodles; return to oven for 5 minutes. Makes 10 to 12 servings.

Betty Lou Wright
Hendersonville, TN
If I had a nickel for every time this make-ahead casserole has been carried to a potluck, I'd be a wealthy woman!

Parmesan Scalloped Potatoes

2 lbs. Yukon Gold potatoes,
  thinly sliced
3 c. whipping cream
1/4 c. fresh parsley, chopped
2 cloves garlic, chopped
1-1/2 t. salt
1/4 t. pepper
1/3 c. grated Parmesan cheese

Layer potatoes in a lightly greased
13"x9" baking pan. In a bowl, stir
together remaining ingredients
except cheese; pour over potatoes.
Bake, uncovered, at 400 degrees
for 30 minutes, stirring gently every
10 minutes. Sprinkle with cheese;
bake again for about 15 minutes, or
until bubbly and golden. Let stand
10 minutes before serving. Serves 8.

Tina Goodpasture
Meadowview, VA

Whether you eat them hot,
cold or warm...these are some
great scalloped potatoes!

Hearty Tortilla Casserole

2 lbs. ground beef
1 onion, chopped
2 t. instant coffee granules
1 t. salt
1 t. pepper
1 T. chili powder
29-oz. can tomato sauce, divided
12 10-inch flour tortillas
1/2 c. cream cheese, softened
1/3 c. water
2 c. shredded Cheddar or
    mozzarella cheese
12 black olives, sliced

Brown beef and onion in a skillet over medium heat; drain. Add coffee granules, seasonings and half the tomato sauce to beef mixture; set aside. Spread each tortilla with cream cheese. Add 1/4 cup of beef mixture to each tortilla and fold over. Place folded tortillas in a greased 13"x9" baking pan. Top with any remaining beef mixture. In a bowl, combine water and remaining tomato sauce; drizzle over tortillas. Sprinkle cheese and olives on top. Cover with aluminum foil and bake at 375 degrees for about 25 minutes, until heated through. Serves 6 to 8.

Angela Murphy
Tempe, AZ

A hint of coffee brings a warm heartiness to this dish!

Famous Calico Beans

1 lb. ground beef
1/4 lb. bacon, chopped
1 onion, chopped
16-oz. can pork & beans
15-oz. can kidney beans, drained
  and liquid reserved
15-oz. can butter beans, drained
  and liquid reserved
1/2 c. catsup
1/2 c. brown sugar, packed
2 T. vinegar
1/2 t. salt

Brown beef, bacon and onion in a
large skillet over medium heat; drain.
Spread beans in a lightly greased
13"x9" baking pan; add beef mixture.
In a bowl, combine remaining
ingredients; pour over beef mixture.
If more liquid is needed, add
reserved liquid from beans. Bake,
uncovered, at 350 degrees for
one hour. Serves 8.

Barbara Harman
Petersburg, WV
We always enjoy these beans
at our church get-togethers.
No matter who brings them,
they're always a hit.

Peg's Tomato-Bacon Pie

2 to 3 tomatoes, peeled
    and sliced
9-inch pie crust, baked
salt and pepper to taste
1/2 c. green onions, chopped
1/3 c. fresh basil, chopped
1/2 c. bacon, crisply cooked
    and crumbled
1 c. mayonnaise
1 c. shredded Cheddar cheese

Layer tomato slices in pie crust.
Season to taste with salt and pepper.
Top with onions, basil and bacon.
In a bowl, mix together mayonnaise
and cheese; spread over bacon. Bake,
uncovered, at 350 degrees for
30 minutes, or until lightly golden.
Serves 6 to 8.

Peggy Buckshaw
Stow, OH

This scrumptious pie
will be a hit at your
next get-together!

Ham & Cheese Strata

12 slices bread, crusts removed
1 lb. cooked ham, diced
2 c. shredded Cheddar cheese
6 eggs, beaten
3 c. milk
2 t. Worcestershire sauce
1 t. dry mustard
1/2 t. salt
1/4 t. pepper
1/8 t. cayenne pepper
1/4 c. onion, minced
1/4 c. green pepper, minced
1/4 c. butter, melted
1 c. corn flake cereal, crushed

Arrange 6 slices of bread in a single layer in a greased 13"x9" baking pan; top with ham and cheese. Cover with remaining bread. In a bowl, beat eggs, milk, Worcestershire sauce and seasonings. Stir in onion and green pepper; pour over bread mixture. Cover and refrigerate overnight. Remove from the refrigerator 30 minutes before baking. Drizzle butter over casserole; sprinkle with cereal. Bake, uncovered, at 350 degrees for about one hour, or until a knife inserted near the center comes out clean. Let stand 10 minutes before serving. Serves 8 to 10.

Mary Gage
Wakewood, CA
The crushed corn flake cereal adds a wonderful crunch to this classic make-ahead casserole!

Supreme Pizza Casserole

16-oz. pkg. rotini pasta,
   uncooked
2 15-oz. jars pizza sauce
2-1/4 oz. can sliced black olives,
   drained
4-oz. can sliced mushrooms,
   drained
1 green pepper, chopped
1 onion, chopped
20 to 30 pepperoni slices
2 c. shredded pizza-blend or
   Italian-blend cheese

Cook pasta according to package
directions; drain. Combine pasta
with remaining ingredients except
cheese. Transfer to a 13"x9" baking
pan; top with cheese. Bake,
uncovered, at 425 degrees for
20 to 25 minutes, until cheese is
golden and bubbly. Serves 8 to 10.

75

Tasha Petenzi
Goodlettsville, TN

This is a great recipe
for a potluck dinner or
an easy weeknight supper.

Mexican Braid

1 lb. ground turkey
10-oz. can diced tomatoes with
    green chiles, drained
1 onion, chopped
1 c. corn
2 loaves frozen bread dough,
    thawed
8-oz. pkg. shredded Pepper Jack
    cheese

Brown turkey with tomatoes and onion in a skillet over medium heat; drain. Add corn; cook until heated through. Roll out each loaf of dough to 1/4-inch thickness. Transfer to baking sheets that have been lined with lightly greased aluminum foil. Cut diagonal slits along each side of the dough, about one inch apart and 3 inches deep. Place half of turkey mixture in the center of each piece of dough. Top each with half of cheese. Fold in short sides of dough, pinching to seal. Fold dough flaps over the turkey mixture, alternating sides and creating a braided pattern. Pinch edges to seal. Bake at 350 degrees for 25 to 30 minutes, until golden. Serves 16.

Kristin Stone
Davis, CA

This is a recipe I created for my husband. He loves spicy foods, and this braid hit the spot!

Cabbage Roll Casserole

2 lbs. ground beef, browned
1 c. onion, chopped
29-oz. can tomato sauce
1 head cabbage, chopped
1 c. instant rice, uncooked
1 t. salt
14-oz. can beef broth

Combine all ingredients except broth in an ungreased, deep 13"x9" baking pan. Drizzle with broth; cover with aluminum foil. Bake at 350 degrees for one hour; uncover and stir. Cover again; bake 30 additional minutes, or until rice is cooked and casserole is heated through. Makes 10 to 12 servings.

77

Dianne Gregory
Sheridan, AR

The flavors of a tasty favorite without all the fuss!

Pierogie Casserole

4 onions, chopped
6 T. butter, divided
10 potatoes, peeled and boiled
1/2 c. chicken broth
1/2 to 1 c. milk
salt and pepper to taste
2 eggs, beaten
1/4 c. shredded Colby cheese
1/2 c. shredded Cheddar cheese, divided
16-oz. pkg. mafalda or bowtie pasta, cooked

In a skillet over medium heat, sauté onions in 2 tablespoons butter; set aside. Mash potatoes with remaining butter, broth, milk, salt and pepper. Add eggs and cheeses, reserving some cheese for topping; mix well. Layer pasta, potato mixture and onion in a greased 13"x9" baking pan. Top with remaining cheese. Bake, uncovered, at 350 degrees for 30 minutes, or until heated through. Serves 12.

Cheryl Lagler
Zionsville, PA

Mafalda pasta is perfect in this recipe if you have it handy in the pantry.

Chicken Chestnut Casserole

6 boneless, skinless chicken
   breasts
1 t. salt
8-oz. can sliced water chestnuts,
   drained
2 10-3/4 oz. cans cream of
   mushroom soup
12-oz. pkg. shredded Cheddar
   cheese
2-oz. jar diced pimentos,
   drained
1 c. milk
7-oz. pkg. elbow macaroni,
   uncooked
1 onion, finely chopped

Cover chicken with water in a medium saucepan; bring to a boil over medium-high heat. Add salt and simmer until chicken is tender. Drain, reserving 1-1/2 cups broth from the saucepan. Cube chicken; set aside. Mix remaining ingredients and reserved broth in a large bowl. Fold in chicken and spread mixture in a lightly greased 13"x9" baking pan. Cover and refrigerate for at least 12 hours. Bake, uncovered, at 325 degrees for one hour and 15 minutes. Serves 8 to 10.

Nancy Molldrem
Eau Claire, WI

A great make-ahead dish...pure comfort food at its finest.

Turkey & Wild Rice Quiche

1 c. wild rice, uncooked
1/3 c. green onions, chopped
1/4 c. red pepper, chopped
5 T. butter
10-inch deep-dish pie crust
1/2 lb. deli smoked turkey, diced
2 c. shredded Swiss cheese
6 eggs, beaten
1 c. half-and-half
1 T. Worcestershire sauce

Cook rice according to package directions; set aside. Sauté onions and red pepper in butter over medium heat until crisp-tender. In pie crust, layer turkey, onion mixture, cheese and rice. In a bowl, whisk together remaining ingredients; pour over rice. Bake, uncovered, at 400 degrees for 20 minutes. Reduce heat to 325 degrees and bake an additional 30 to 35 minutes. Remove from oven; let stand 15 minutes before cutting into wedges. Serves 6 to 8.

Angela Biggin
Lyons, IL

The combination of turkey and wild rice is a pleasant change from a traditional quiche.

Chile Relleno Casserole

7-oz. can whole green chiles, drained
16-oz. pkg. shredded Monterey Jack cheese, divided
16-oz. pkg. shredded Cheddar cheese, divided
7-oz. can chopped green chiles
salt and pepper to taste
6 eggs, beaten
13-oz. can evaporated milk
Optional: salsa and sour cream

Slit whole chiles and remove seeds; rinse and dry. Lay whole chiles, skin-side down, in a lightly greased 13"x9" baking pan; sprinkle with half of each cheese. Top with chopped chiles, remaining cheese, salt and pepper. In a bowl, combine eggs and milk; pour over top. Bake, uncovered, at 350 degrees for 45 minutes. Serve with salsa or sour cream, if desired. Serves 8.

81

**Georgia Mallory
Fullerton, CA**

This is a tasty breakfast, brunch or anytime casserole...yummy served with sour cream, salsa and lots of fresh melon!

Quick Beefy Bean & Biscuit Bake

1 lb. ground beef
1/2 c. onion, chopped
1 t. salt
1/2 t. pepper
28-oz. can brown sugar baked
 beans
1/4 c. barbecue sauce
1/4 c. catsup
1 c. shredded Cheddar cheese
16.3-oz. tube refrigerated
 buttermilk biscuits

In a skillet over medium heat, brown beef with onion, salt and pepper; drain. Stir in baked beans, barbecue sauce and catsup; spoon beef mixture into an ungreased 13"x9" baking pan. Sprinkle cheese evenly over top. Separate each biscuit into 2 thinner biscuits and arrange evenly on top. Bake, uncovered, at 350 degrees for 30 to 35 minutes, until bubbly and biscuits are golden. Makes 6 to 8 servings.

Hana Brosmer
Huntingburg, IN
Golden biscuits layered over a hearty filling make this meal satisfying.

Cheesy Chile Rice

2 c. water
2 c. instant rice, uncooked
16-oz. container sour cream
4-oz. can diced green chiles
3 c. shredded Cheddar cheese,
  divided

In a saucepan over medium-high heat, bring water to a boil. Stir in rice; remove from heat. Cover and let stand 5 minutes, until water is absorbed. In a large bowl, mix together rice, sour cream, chiles and 2 cups cheese. Spread in a greased 2-quart casserole dish; top with remaining cheese. Bake, uncovered, at 400 degrees for 30 minutes, or until cheese is melted and top is lightly golden. Makes 6 servings.

83

Wendy Reaume
Ontario, Canada

When I was growing up, my mom made this simple rice dish whenever we had Mexican food for dinner. It's yummy with burritos and tortilla chips.

Rumbledethumps

1 lb. potatoes, peeled and diced
2 T. butter
1 onion, thinly sliced
2 c. cabbage, finely shredded
salt and pepper to taste
2/3 c. shredded Cheddar cheese,
   divided

Cover potatoes with water in a
saucepan; bring to a boil. Reduce
heat; cover and simmer for
8 minutes, or until just tender.
Drain and rinse under cold water;
drain again. Transfer potatoes to a
bowl; mash coarsely with a fork and
set aside. Heat butter in a skillet;
add onion and cook over low heat
for 10 minutes, or until soft. Add
cabbage; cook for 5 minutes. Stir in
potatoes, salt and pepper. Remove
from heat; stir in 2 tablespoons
cheese. Transfer to a greased
9"x9" baking pan; sprinkle with
remaining cheese. Bake, uncovered,
at 350 degrees for 20 minutes, or
until heated through. Serves 4 to 6.

Jane Finn
Gurnee, IL

A funny Scottish name for
a hearty, satisfying side!
Garnish with some crispy
bacon to make it even better!

Warm & Wonderful Chicken Salad

2 c. cooked chicken, shredded
2 c. celery, diced
1 T. onion, grated
1 c. mayonnaise
1/2 c. slivered almonds
1/2 t. lemon juice
1-1/2 c. shredded Cheddar
   cheese, divided
1/2 c. potato chips, crushed

Mix chicken, celery, onion, mayonnaise, almonds, lemon juice and one cup cheese in a greased 13"x9" baking pan. Top with remaining cheese and chips. Bake, uncovered, at 450 degrees for 15 to 20 minutes, until hot and bubbly. Serves 6 to 8.

Susan Fracker
New Concord, OH

Perfect paired with fresh fruit and a warm muffin.

Mushroom & Barley Casserole

3/4 c. quick-cooking barley,
  uncooked
1/2 c. onion, chopped
1/4 c. butter
4-oz. can sliced mushrooms
14-1/2 oz. can chicken broth
1/2 c. sliced almonds

In a saucepan, sauté barley and
onion in butter until golden; spoon
into a greased 1-1/2 quart casserole
dish. Add undrained mushrooms
and broth; mix well. Bake, covered,
at 350 degrees for one hour and
15 minutes. Remove cover and
sprinkle with almonds. Bake,
uncovered, for an additional
15 minutes. Serves 4 to 6.

Anne Marie Verdiramo
Rochester, MN
My family loves this recipe!
It was even published
in my grandmother's
church cookbook.

Green Bean Delight

4 16-oz. cans green beans,
   drained
1-oz. pkg. ranch salad dressing
   mix
2 10-3/4 oz. cans cream of
   mushroom soup
1/4 c. milk
8-oz. pkg. shredded Colby Jack
   cheese
1 c. sliced almonds or cashews
2.8-oz. can French fried onions

Place green beans in a lightly
greased 13"x9" baking pan; set aside.
Combine dressing mix, soup and
milk in a bowl; pour over beans.
Sprinkle with cheese and nuts; top
with onions. Bake, uncovered,
at 350 degrees for 25 minutes.
Serves 8 to 10.

Jackie Balla
Walbridge, OH

An old standby dressed
up with shredded cheese
and nuts.

Famous White Mac & Cheese

16-oz. pkg. elbow macaroni,
   uncooked
2 T. butter
2 T. all-purpose flour
3 c. milk
1 lb. Monterey Jack cheese, cubed
1/2 lb. Pepper Jack cheese, cubed

Cook macaroni according to
package directions; drain and set
aside. Meanwhile, melt butter in a
saucepan over medium heat. Stir in
flour until combined; add milk and
stir until mixture boils. Remove
from heat; add cheese and stir until
melted. Combine cheese mixture
and cooked macaroni; place in an
ungreased 13"x9" baking pan. Bake,
uncovered, at 350 degrees for
30 minutes, or until bubbly.
Makes 8 servings.

Shannon James
Georgetown, KY

When my four kids come
running in from playing and
see that my mac & cheese
is in the oven, it puts a
smile on everyone's face.

Game-Day BBQ Onions

11-oz. pkg. mesquite barbecue-
  flavored potato chips, divided
2 10-3/4 oz. cans cream of
  chicken soup
1/2 c. milk
4 sweet onions, thinly sliced
  and divided
2 c. shredded sharp Cheddar
  cheese, divided

Crush 2 cups of potato chips; set aside. Whisk together soup and milk; set aside. Place half of onion slices in the bottom of a 13"x9" baking pan coated with non-stick vegetable spray. Spread uncrushed chips over onions; add one cup cheese and half of soup mixture. Repeat layering. Top with reserved crushed chips. Bake, uncovered, at 350 degrees for one hour. Serves 10.

89

Cheryl Breeden
North Platte, NE

So simple...a true football night party favorite that will turn anyone into an onion lover.

Hashbrown Casserole

10-3/4 oz. can cream of
chicken soup
8-oz. container sour cream
1/2 c. margarine, melted and
divided
2 c. shredded sharp Cheddar
cheese
salt and pepper to taste
30-oz. pkg. frozen shredded
hashbrowns, thawed
1 c. corn flake cereal, crushed

In a bowl, combine soup, sour
cream, half the margarine, shredded
cheese, salt and pepper. Pour mixture
into a lightly greased 13"x9" baking
pan; top with hashbrowns. Mix
corn flake cereal and remaining
margarine; spread over hashbrowns.
Bake, uncovered, at 350 degrees for
30 minutes, or until hot and bubbly.
Serves 6.

Shelia Butts
Creedmoor, NC

Such a creamy, filling
side dish and it's
so easy to make.

Kale & Potato Casserole

1/4 c. butter, melted
3 potatoes, thinly sliced
10 leaves kale, finely chopped
5 T. grated Parmesan cheese
salt and pepper to taste

In a bowl, drizzle butter over potatoes and mix well. Grease a cast-iron skillet and arrange a layer of potatoes in the bottom. Top with 1/3 of the kale, 1/3 of the cheese, salt and pepper. Continue layering, ending with potatoes; sprinkle with remaining cheese. Cover with aluminum foil and bake at 375 degrees for 30 minutes. Remove foil and bake for another 15 to 30 minutes, until potatoes are tender. Serves 4 to 6.

91

Jill Ross
Gooseberry Patch

Warm potatoes, wilted greens and Parmesan cheese make this a hearty side!

Noodle Kugel

16-oz. pkg. wide egg noodles,
    uncooked
3/4 to 1 c. butter, melted
16-oz. container sour cream
20-oz. can crushed pineapple,
    drained
4 eggs, beaten
1 c. sugar
1/2 t. salt
2 t. vanilla extract
Optional: cinnamon

Cook noodles according to package
directions; drain. Combine noodles
and remaining ingredients in a
greased 13"x9" baking pan. Bake,
uncovered, at 350 degrees for one
hour, or until heated through. Top
with cinnamon, if using. Serves
10 to 12.

Gail Flusche-Hill
Hammond, IN

My whole family loves this
sweet dish... it's always
a hit every holiday!

White Cheddar-Cauliflower Casserole

1 head cauliflower, cooked and
   mashed
8-oz. pkg. shredded white
   Cheddar cheese, divided
1/2 lb. bacon, crisply cooked,
   crumbled and divided
1/2 c. cream cheese, softened
2 T. sour cream
salt and pepper to taste

Combine cauliflower, half the
Cheddar cheese and 3/4 of the bacon
in a bowl. Add cream cheese and sour
cream; mix well. Spread mixture in a
greased 8"x8" baking pan; top with
remaining cheese and bacon.
Sprinkle with salt and pepper. Bake,
uncovered, at 350 degrees for 20 to
25 minutes, until bubbly and golden
around edges. Serves 6.

93

Lisa Ashton
Aston, PA

Lots of cheese and bacon
will have the kids eating
their cauliflower in this
terrific casserole.

Scalloped Potatoes

3 potatoes, peeled and sliced
6 slices bacon, halved
1 onion, chopped
3 T. fried chicken coating mix
1/2 t. salt
2 c. milk
1 c. shredded Cheddar cheese

In a saucepan over medium heat,
cover potatoes with water and
cook until almost tender; drain.
Meanwhile, cook bacon and onion
in a skillet over medium heat. Drain,
reserving 2 tablespoons drippings.
Add coating mix, salt and milk to
reserved drippings; cook until
thickened. Fold potatoes into bacon
mixture. Transfer to a greased
3-1/2 quart casserole dish and bake,
covered, at 350 degrees for
30 minutes. Remove cover, top
with cheese and bake for another
15 minutes, or until cheese is melted.
Serves 6.

Lynnette Zaunmiller
San Tan Valley, AZ

My mother used to make this
recipe quite often...there
were three of us girls
and we all loved it!

Golden Macaroni & Cheese

10-3/4 oz. can cream of
    mushroom soup
1/2 c. milk
1/2 t. mustard
1/8 t. pepper
3 c. elbow macaroni, cooked
2 c. shredded Cheddar cheese,
    divided
1 c. French fried onions

Blend soup, milk, mustard and
pepper in a lightly greased 1-1/2 quart
casserole dish. Stir in macaroni and
1-1/2 cups cheese. Bake, uncovered,
at 350 degrees for 20 minutes. Top
with remaining cheese and onions;
bake 10 additional minutes. Serves 4.

95

Gale Harris
Fort Worth, TX

A topping of crispy
French fried onions gives
this traditional standby
extra crunch!

Butternut Squash Casserole

1 to 2 butternut squash, peeled
   and cubed
2 eggs, beaten
1/4 c. milk
2 T. butter, softened
1/2 c. sugar
1 t. vanilla
1/2 t. cinnamon
1/2 t. nutmeg

In a saucepan over medium-high
heat, cover squash with water and
cook until tender, about 7 to
9 minutes; drain. In a small bowl,
beat squash until smooth. Add
remaining ingredients; beat well.
Spoon into a 2-quart casserole dish
coated with non-stick vegetable spray.
Cover and bake at 350 degrees for
30 to 35 minutes, until heated
through. Serves 4 to 6.

Mary Patenaude
Griswold, CT

This is a wonderfully
yummy addition to any meal.
We especially love it
around the holidays.

Cheesy Vegetable Casserole

2 16-oz. pkgs. frozen stir-fry
  blend vegetables, thawed
  and drained
16-oz. pkg. pasteurized process
  cheese spread
1/4 c. milk
1/2 c. butter
1 sleeve round buttery crackers,
  crushed

Place vegetables in a lightly greased
13"x9" baking pan; set aside. Melt
cheese in a saucepan over low heat;
add milk. Stir until smooth; pour
over vegetables. Melt butter and stir
in cracker crumbs; sprinkle over
vegetables. Bake, uncovered, at
350 degrees for 20 to 25 minutes,
until heated through. Makes 6 to
8 servings.

Colleen McAleavey
Plum, PA

We like to vary this
casserole by choosing
different blends of
frozen vegetables.

Scalloped Corn

1 onion, chopped
1/2 c. plus 1 T. butter, melted
14-3/4 oz. can creamed corn
2 11-oz. cans corn, drained
8-1/2 oz. pkg. corn muffin mix
dried parsley
salt and pepper to taste

In a skillet over medium heat, sauté onion in butter until translucent. Combine onion and remaining ingredients in a lightly greased 13"x9" baking pan. Bake, uncovered, at 350 degrees for 45 minutes to one hour, until golden. Serves 8.

Barbara Pache
Marshall, WI

Grandmother made this casserole for every family reunion. It was always everyone's favorite.

Cheesy Lentils & Rice Casserole

3/4 c. dried lentils, uncooked
1/2 c. long-cooking rice,
    uncooked
3 c. chicken broth
2 T. dried, minced onion
1/2 t. dried basil
1/4 t. dried oregano
1/4 t. dried thyme
1/4 t. garlic powder
3/4 c. shredded Cheddar cheese

Blend all ingredients except cheese
in a 2-quart casserole dish. Bake,
covered, at 300 degrees for one hour
and 15 minutes. Uncover and top
with cheese; bake for 15 minutes, or
until cheese is melted. Serves 4 to 6.

99

Shirley Howie
Foxboro, MA

This is such a delicious
low-fat casserole.
My husband requests it
all the time!

Spinach Casserole

2 10-oz. pkgs. frozen chopped
    spinach, thawed and drained
salt and pepper to taste
10-3/4 oz. can cream of
    mushroom soup
8-oz. container sour cream
3/4 c. frozen chopped pepper,
    onion & celery mix
1/2 sleeve round buttery
    crackers, crushed
3 eggs, beaten
2 c. shredded Cheddar cheese,
    divided

Place spinach in a large bowl; season
with salt and pepper. Combine
remaining ingredients, reserving
1/2 cup cheese. Pour mixture into a
lightly greased 2-quart casserole dish.
Bake, uncovered, at 350 degrees for
45 minutes, or until center is set.
Top with remaining cheese. Bake for
an additional 10 minutes, or until
cheese is melted. Serves 8 to 10.

Kay Daugherty
Collinsville, MS
This yummy casserole
is expected at every
family gathering!

Broccoli & Rice Casserole

1 c. long-cooking rice, uncooked
1 onion, chopped
3 stalks celery, chopped
1 c. butter, divided
10-oz. pkg. frozen chopped
   broccoli, thawed and drained
16-oz. jar pasteurized process
   cheese sauce
10-3/4 oz. can cream of
   mushroom soup
1 c. sour cream
1 sleeve round buttery crackers,
   crushed

Cook rice according to package
directions; set aside. Sauté onion
and celery for 3 minutes in 1/2 cup
butter. Mix all ingredients except
remaining butter and crackers in a
greased 2-quart casserole dish; top
with crackers. Melt remaining butter
and drizzle over crackers. Bake,
uncovered, at 350 degrees for
35 minutes, or until heated
through. Serves 8.

101

Patricia Elmore
Bessemer City, NC
I have been cooking this
dish for my family for
over 40 years, and they still
get excited to see this
loved dish on the table.

Minnesota Carrot-Asparagus Bake

1-1/2 c. carrots, peeled and
    chopped
1 c. onion, sliced
16-oz. jar pasteurized process
    cheese sauce
3 T. butter, melted
3 T. all-purpose flour
1-1/2 c. milk
1 t. salt
1 t. pepper
10-oz. pkg. frozen asparagus,
    thawed and drained
2.8-oz. can French fried onions

Combine carrots and onion in a
saucepan. Cover with water and boil
until almost tender; drain and set
aside. In a bowl, mix together cheese
sauce, butter, flour and milk; add salt
and pepper. Set aside. Layer carrot
mixture and asparagus in a greased
9"x9" baking pan; drizzle cheese
mixture over top. Sprinkle with
onions. Bake, uncovered, at
350 degrees for 15 to 20 minutes,
until heated through. Serves 8.

Mary Scurti
Highland, CA
We make this yummy
casserole year 'round, but
it is definitely a tradition
at our holiday table.

Sweet Potato-Apple Bake

4 sweet potatoes, boiled, peeled
   and sliced
1/2 c. butter
1/2 c. sugar
1/2 c. brown sugar, packed
1 to 2 t. cinnamon
4 tart apples, peeled, cored
   and sliced
1/2 c. water
1/4 c. lemon juice
1/4 c. orange juice

Arrange a layer of sliced potatoes
in a greased one-quart casserole dish;
dot with butter and sprinkle with
sugar, brown sugar and cinnamon.
Arrange a layer of apple slices on
top; continue layering until all
ingredients except water and juices
are used. Combine water and juices;
pour over top. Cover and bake at
400 degrees for 45 minutes, or
until apples are tender. Makes 4 to
6 servings.

103

Wendy Jacobs
Idaho Falls, ID

This is a really tasty
change from the traditional
sweet potato casseroles
we're used to.

Savory Rice Casserole

4-oz. can sliced mushrooms,
   drained and liquid reserved
8-oz. can sliced water chestnuts,
   drained and liquid reserved
1/2 c. butter
1 c. long-cooking rice, uncooked
10-1/2 oz. can French onion
   soup

In a skillet over medium heat, sauté
mushrooms and water chestnuts in
butter; set aside. Add uncooked rice
to an ungreased one-quart casserole
dish. Stir in soup, mushroom
mixture and reserved liquids. Bake,
covered, at 375 degrees for 45 to
60 minutes, until rice is tender.
Serves 6 to 8.

Kathy Dassel
Newburgh, IN

My sister-in-law gave me
this delicious recipe while
we were visiting her in
Raleigh, North Carolina.

Pineapple Casserole

20-oz. can crushed pineapple
20-oz. can pineapple chunks,
    drained
2 c. shredded sharp Cheddar
    cheese
1/4 c. sugar
6 T. all-purpose flour
1 sleeve round buttery crackers,
    crushed
1/2 c. butter, melted
Optional: pineapple rings,
    maraschino cherries

Mix together all ingredients except
crackers and butter in a greased
13"x9" baking pan. Top with
crackers; drizzle butter over top.
Bake, uncovered, at 350 degrees for
about 30 minutes, or until heated
through and bubbly. Garnish with
pineapple rings and cherries, if
desired. Serves 8.

Lynn Filipowicz
Wilmington, NC

I have been making this
dish for years...it's good
hot or cold.

Fabulous Baked Potato Casserole

6 to 7 potatoes, peeled and cubed
2 c. shredded Cheddar cheese
1 c. mayonnaise
1/2 c. sour cream
1 onion, diced
6 slices bacon, crisply cooked
   and crumbled

In a large saucepan, boil potatoes
in water until fork-tender, about
20 minutes; drain and set aside to
cool. Combine cheese, mayonnaise,
sour cream and onion; mix in
potatoes, tossing gently to coat.
Spread potato mixture in a buttered
13"x9" baking pan; sprinkle bacon on
top. Bake, uncovered, at 350 degrees
until golden and bubbly, about 20 to
25 minutes. Serves 8.

Ginia Johnston
Greeneville, TN
Make sure to get some quick,
because this delectable dish
always disappears first
at every gathering!

Zucchini-Corn Casserole

3 lbs. zucchini, cubed
2 c. corn
1 onion, chopped
1 green pepper, chopped
2 T. butter
salt and pepper to taste
4 eggs, lightly beaten
1 c. shredded Cheddar cheese
paprika to taste

In a saucepan, cook zucchini in boiling water for 2 to 3 minutes; drain and set aside. In a skillet over medium heat, sauté corn, onion and green pepper in butter until crisp-tender. Remove from heat and add zucchini to corn mixture; season with salt and pepper and let cool slightly. Stir in eggs and transfer to a greased 13"x9" baking pan. Top with cheese and paprika. Bake, uncovered, at 350 degrees for 40 minutes, or until lightly golden and bubbly. Serves 6 to 8.

Dani Simmers
Kendallville, IN

This recipe came from my friend's great-aunt...it tastes wonderful and is pretty easy to fix, too!

INDEX

INDEX

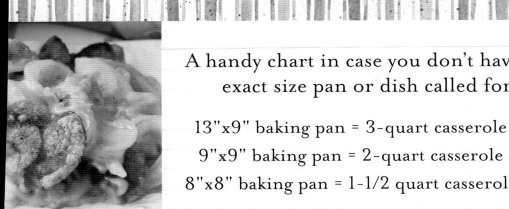

A handy chart in case you don't have the exact size pan or dish called for:

13"x9" baking pan = 3-quart casserole dish

9"x9" baking pan = 2-quart casserole dish

8"x8" baking pan = 1-1/2 quart casserole dish

ne-Day BBQ Onions, page 89

Curry Chicken Casserole, page 67

Scalloped Potatoes, page 94

Pineapple Casserole, page 105

Taco-Filled Pasta Shells, page 35

Sweet Corn & Rice Casserole, page 58

Our Story

Back in 1984, we were next-door neighbors raising our families in the little town of Delaware, Ohio. Two moms with small children, we were looking for a way to do what we loved and stay home with the kids too. We had always shared a love of home cooking and making memories with family & friends and so, after many a conversation over the backyard fence, **Gooseberry Patch** was born.

We put together our first catalog at our kitchen tables, enlisting the help of our loved ones wherever we could. From that very first mailing, we found an immediate connection with many of our customers and it wasn't long before we began receiving letters, photos and recipes from these new friends. In 1992, we put together our very first cookbook, compiled from hundreds of these recipes and, the rest, as they say, is history.

Hard to believe it's been over 25 years since those kitchen-table days! From that original little **Gooseberry Patch** family, we've grown to include an amazing group of creative folks who love cooking, decorating and creating as much as we do. Today, we're best known for our homestyle, family-friendly cookbooks, now recognized as national bestsellers.

One thing's for sure, we couldn't have done it without our friends all across the country. Each year, we're honored to turn thousands of your recipes into our collectible cookbooks. Our hope is that each book captures the stories and heart of all of you who have shared with us. Whether you've been with us since the beginning or are just discovering us, welcome to the **Gooseberry Patch** family!

JoAnn & Vickie

Visit us online:
www.gooseberrypatch.com
1•800•854•6673

U.S. to Canadian Recipe Equivalents

Volume Measurements

1/4 teaspoon	1 mL
1/2 teaspoon	2 mL
1 teaspoon	5 mL
1 tablespoon = 3 teaspoons	15 mL
2 tablespoons = 1 fluid ounce	30 mL
1/4 cup	60 mL
1/3 cup	75 mL
1/2 cup = 4 fluid ounces	125 mL
1 cup = 8 fluid ounces	250 mL
2 cups = 1 pint =16 fluid ounces	500 mL
4 cups = 1 quart	1 L

Weights

1 ounce	30 g
4 ounces	120 g
8 ounces	225 g
16 ounces = 1 pound	450 g

Oven Temperatures

300° F	150° C
325° F	160° C
350° F	180° C
375° F	190° C
400° F	200° C
450° F	230° C

Baking Pan Sizes

Square

8x8x2 inches	2 L = 20x20x5 cm
9x9x2 inches	2.5 L = 23x23x5 cm

Rectangular

13x9x2 inches	3.5 L = 33x23x5 cm

Loaf

9x5x3 inches	2 L = 23x13x7 cm

Round

8x1-1/2 inches	1.2 L = 20x4 cm
9x1-1/2 inches	1.5 L = 23x4 cm

Recipe Abbreviations

t. = teaspoon	ltr. = liter
T. = tablespoon	oz. = ounce
c. = cup	lb. = pound
pt. = pint	doz. = dozen
qt. = quart	pkg. = package
gal. = gallon	env. = envelope

Kitchen Measurements

A pinch = 1/8 tablespoon	1 fluid ounce = 2 tablespoons
3 teaspoons = 1 tablespoon	4 fluid ounces = 1/2 cup
2 tablespoons = 1/8 cup	8 fluid ounces = 1 cup
4 tablespoons = 1/4 cup	16 fluid ounces = 1 pint
8 tablespoons = 1/2 cup	32 fluid ounces = 1 quart
16 tablespoons = 1 cup	16 ounces net weight = 1 pound
2 cups = 1 pint	
4 cups = 1 quart	
4 quarts = 1 gallon	